THE COVENANT OF MARRIAGE

Courtney M. Gardner

Cover designed by Tammie T. Polk
Art: Unsplash

Courtney M. Gardner
Visit my website at www.amazon.com/author/courtneygardner

Printed in the United States of America

First Printing: November 2023
Amazon/KDP

ISBN-13 979-8-218-37589-8

CONTENTS

ISRAEL SET THE EXAMPLE OF HAVING THE
PERFECT MARRIAGE.... UNTIL LAWLESSNESS
OVERRULED GOD'S PLAN.
—COURTNEY M. GARDNER

"MARRIAGE IS NOT A SPRINT, BUT A MARATHON"
--ANONYMOUS

MARRIAGE IS THE THEME OF THE HOLY BIBLE AT
THE BEGINNING OF GENESIS IT ENLIGHTENS WITH
THE FIRST MAN AND WOMAN AND IT FINISHED   AT
THE END OF REVELATIONS WITH THE MARRIAGE
OF OUR MESSIAH AND HIS BRIDE (THE CHURCH)

INTRODUCTION

It may surprise many to learn that the Bible is primarily the Book concerning the Nation of Israel and that most other nations are mentioned only as they encountered Israel. Starting from Adam to Abraham, God created the first humans physically perfect.

The spiritual character of God was yet to be built into Adam and Eve and those who would spring from them.

Adam and Eve rejected the Tree of Life and, by rejecting the Tree of Life, they chose instead Satan's "get" way of life – the self-centered way of vanity, jealousy, and competition leading to strife and destruction.

God shut the first humans and their descendants off from the Holy Spirit except for those few Gods specially called to Christ.

The second Adam began His reign on earth and all the minds of men are open to God's spiritual truth.

As men began to multiply on the earth, all of Adam's sons except one followed in his Satan-inspired course of human nature.

Before Abraham, only three men are mentioned in the Bible as following God's way of life.

The first person Jesus Christ called righteous was Abel (Matthew 23:35). The other two who walked with God were Enoch and Noah (Genesis 5:22, 6:9).

Shem was the direct ancestor of Abraham. He may have continued for some time in the knowledge or worship of God, but there is no record of his or anyone else "walking with God" from the line to Noah until Abram.

God told Abram to leave his relatives and land unknown to a place of blessings (Genesis 12:1-3). Abram obeyed God without any questions (Genesis 12:4). God promised that, from Abraham, there would be nations and kings. God also reconfirmed the same promises to Isaac, Abraham's son (Genesis 26:1-5) and Jacob's sons (Genesis 27:26-29). Jacob, whose name meant "supplanter," was later changed to Israel (Genesis 35:10).

Methods and Problems

Israel, whose previous name was Jacob, had twelve sons.

His favorite son, Joseph, was sold into slavery by his brothers.

Joseph was taken to Egypt and soon became a ruler second to Pharaoh.

A great famine caused Israel to send his sons to Egypt to buy food, where they became reacquainted with Joseph (Genesis 45:9, 17-18).

The place where they settled was in Goshen (Genesis 46:28).

After Joseph's death, another Pharaoh who didn't know Joseph made slaves of the children of Israel and made their lives bitter (Exodus 1:8-14).

God chose Moses to lead the children of Israel out of Egypt. Moses was trained for this mission as a prince in the palace of the Egyptian Pharaoh (Exodus 2:1-10). God also allowed Aaron to be Moses' spokesperson (Exodus 4:10-16).

God turned the Egyptian's gods and objects of worship against them to show that they were not active, living gods.

The children of Israel finally left Egypt at Pharaoh's command.

Once gone, Pharaoh changed his mind and went after Israel with his army.

When they reached the Red Sea, the children of Israel were trapped. Pharaoh's army was not too far behind them. The children of Israel stood there helpless.

In Egypt, God had caused Israel's release by supernatural plagues.

Now, God caused the water of the Red Sea to roll back to form a wall of water. The Israelites walked through.

On the opposite side, the children of Israel looked and saw Pharaoh and his army coming after them. God allowed the waters to collapse upon them, drowning the Egyptian army.

Israel then went toward Mount Sinai where God had them set up a camp.

Defining Marriage

One of the most important doctrines the living Christ has revealed to His Church is that of the Old and New Covenants.

Many confuse the word covenant with testament.

A testament is not a covenant, and a covenant is not a testament.

According to the American Heritage Dictionary, the word "testament" is a legal document providing for the disposition of personal property after death.

"Covenant" means a formal binding agreement, compact, or contract.

In Biblical usage, a covenant is a contract, or agreement, in which one party promises certain rewards or payments in return for certain stipulations by the other party.

Through Moses, God proposed a covenant with the Israelites (Exodus 19:3–6).

God promised to make them a great nation if they would obey Him. The people gladly agreed in verse eight, "...all that the Lord hath spoken we will do" they promised.

They were so certain of their ability to obey God that they affirmed to abide by the covenant.

The Lord told Moses to tell the children of Israel that He would come down on the third day (Exodus 20:1-26, Deuteronomy 5:6-21).

On the third day came an awesome display of lightning, thunder, and thick clouds swirling over the mountain.

God's powerful voice thundered in their ears the basic law, God's way of life.

This covenant made at Sinai, called the Old Covenant today, imposed upon the people of Israel certain terms and conditions to be performed.

The people were to obey the Ten Commandments, and the rewards for obedience would make Israel a nation of high greatness.

Israel agreed before God that they would obey all the laws of the covenant (Exodus 24:3,7). Afterwards, it was sealed in blood (Exodus 24:6-8).

Anything appearing beneath the signature is not legally any part of the covenant.

The covenant made at Sinai was a good example of a marriage covenant between a man and a woman.

As the Lord who dealt with the Old Testament, Israel – the husband – promised to provide for and protect the nation of Israel. The nation—as the wife – agreed to remain faithful to Him and refrain from any adulterous or whorish relations with the gods of other nations.

Israel as a nation accepted the role of a wife to obey her husband (Leviticus 26:1-13, Deuteronomy 28:1-4).

The God of Israel who had redeemed them from the bondage of Egypt revealed His glory to them on Mount Sinai.

He gave His laws to live by and dwelt in their midst.

Imagine the joy that swept over Moses when he saw the plans for the Tabernacle that he was to build and heard the God of the universe would dwell amongst the Israelites (Exodus 25:2, 8-9).

The Tabernacle is of such importance to God's program that fifty chapters of the Bible are given to explain its pattern, construction, and service.

Five names in scripture describe the Tabernacle. It was called a:

- Sanctuary (Exodus 25:8) – denoting that it was set apart for a holy God.
- Tabernacle (Exodus 25:9) – reveals that it was the dwelling place of God among His people.
- Tent (Exodus 26:36) – designated it as a temporary dwelling place of God.
- Tabernacle of the congregation (Exodus 29:42) – it was where God met with His people.

- Tabernacle of Testimony (Exodus 38:21) – described the law given to Moses, which was kept in the Ark of the Covenant in the Holy of Holies.

The Tabernacle stood as a testimony to Israel and the worlds of God's truth and glory.

The institution of the Sabbath in different countries has a long and complex history with explanations given of its origin aside from the divine command.

It was originally connected with the worship of the moon.

There are "many indications in the Hebrew History that the early ancestors of the Israelites were moon worshippers" according to Charles Kent and Jeremiah Jenks.

In the Hebrew religion, the feast of the new moon therefore marked the beginning of the month.

The word "holy" in Hebrew means set apart or distinct.

The Sabbath was to differ from the other days of the week.

Later, Judaism revived the earlier heathen content of the Sabbath and lost sight of its humanitarian significance.

Jesus, with His clear insight into the human heart and needs, with His glowing love said, "The Sabbath was made for man, not man for the Sabbath."

Does the great body of the Christian Church today accept the interpretation of Jesus or that of the early heathenism and later Judaism?

To keep the Sabbath may well be carried out with the same spirit in various ways.

What constitutes theft depends on the law of the state and upon the rights of the property granted by that law, but everywhere the obligations of the individual to God, society, and fellow man remain the same.

Polygamist Converted to Monogamy

God did not sanction polygamy in the Old Testament times.

Abraham was not a polygamist while Sarah, his wife, lived, he never married another woman although Abraham had an illegitimate son by Hagar.

That was an adulterous sin. We can recognize the extenuating circumstances.

Sarah was barren and, for a wife in ancient times, to go childless was felt to be a disgrace.

Hagar slept with Abraham because Sarah allowed it.

Abraham was always obedient to God.

These sins were of the flesh under temptation, not rebellious sins of the heart.

God forgave Abraham's sin of spiritual weakness committed under heavy temptation.

After Sarah's death, Abraham remarried.

Isaac was no polygamist.

There is no mention of any wife for Isaac other than Rebekah.

Isaac's wife Rebekah, like her mother-in-law Sarah, was barren. However, Isaac did not take matters into his own hands and Rebekah did not do as Sarah had done. Isaac trusted God (Genesis 25:21).

We need to trust God to work out our problems.

Jacob had one wife after his conversion, but his name means supplanter.

Jacob received the birthright instead of Esau.

As he bought his brother's birthright, his father-in-law deceived him.

Leah was foisted on Jacob by fraud.

According to the laws of God, Jacob could have rejected her or put her away as soon as he discovered the deception.

He accepted her and wanted another lover as well.

With two wives at the same time, he also had children by their maids.

After Jacob's conversion, God changed his name to Israel, meaning overcomer (Genesis 32:24-30).

God took his second wife, leaving his first and only true wife, Leah (Genesis 35:19).

David repented of polygamy.

He had several wives, but after his serious sin of taking
Bathsheba and having her husband killed, David repented
of the sin (II Samuel 11, 12:9–12).

God forgave David after he repented, but the son died
(Psalm 51).

COMMUNITY VERSUS INDIVIDUAL

Let's look at the four types of marriage:

- Sadiga marriage
- Beena marriage
- Mota marriage
- Levirate marriage

Sadiga Marriage

Marriage between relatives was common since a woman was to marry within the same clan. If she chose to marry outside the clan, she could under certain terms as the clan might permit by their customs or actions.

Compensation was made either to marry and leave the clan or agreed through her father, a male relative of another clan provided she remained with her clan.

This type of marriage is usually governed by the mother but also is used to identify how relationships are to be conducted.

Beena Marriage

Very little is mentioned about the Beena marriage in the Old Testament. This term, Beena marriage, is occasionally used when the children are living with the mother and the husband in his wife's dwelling.

A prime example of the "Beena marriage" is when Moses and Jacob both lived in their wives' homes for a lengthy period (Genesis 29:1-30, Exodus 2:21-22).

Mota Marriage

While the Beena marriage is when the husband dwells in his wife's house for a while, the mota marriage is periodic.

Samson's visits to his wife are a good example of a periodic visit (Judges 15:1).

Samson was very upset about not visiting his wife due to his father-in-law (Judges 15:2).

Levirate Marriage

This term comes from the Latin word "levir" meaning husband's brother.

In ancient Hebrew society, the levirate served to perpetuate the line of the person who died without children.

He is required to marry a brother's widow (Deuteronomy 25:5-10, Ruth 4:5, Genesis 38:8,11).

In non-literate societies, the rights and duties of the first husband still exist, especially with the Sudanese. They consider the children of the first husband to be their biological genitor.

A junior levirate is when the person is much younger than the deceased.

MYSTERY OF LAWLESSNESS

Israel's Unfaithfulness

God chose Israel above all other nations on earth to be His own nation because of His love for and promises to Abraham, Isaac, and Jacob.

They were to set the example of obedience to God for all the other nations to follow (Deuteronomy 4:5-8).

Instead of showing good leadership roles among the nations, they followed the ways and customs of the pagan nations around them.

They failed to become a kingdom of priests and a holy nation (Exodus 19:5-6).

Israel was not offered God's spirit. Only their prophets and appointed leaders were given the Holy Spirit (Numbers 14:24, 1 Peter 1:10-11).

The Israelites did not resist Satan and submit to God.

Ancient Israel did not realize their lack of God's power when they agreed to the terms of the Old Covenant.

They even had problems keeping the letter of the law because, without God's spirit, they were limited in understanding the material knowledge of His spiritual law.

After David's death, his son Solomon succeeded him to the throne of Israel.

Solomon taxed the people mightily and reigned in a gorgeous empire.

He also married Gentile wives.

I don't believe Solomon ever understood the love of only one woman.

Because of his wives, he burned incense and sacrificed to Moloch and other pagan perverted idols (I Kings 11:11–13).

Kingdoms Divided

I Kings 11:26 speaks of Jeroboam, the son of Nabat, an Ephrathite, as Solomon's servant.

Jeroboam was ruler over all the birthright family of God.

God told Solomon, "After his death, the Kingdom will be given to his servant, but not all."

After Jeroboam became king over the house of Israel, he set up the golden calves, introducing idol worship in the kingdom (I Kings 12:28–33).

Sabbath-breaking was the great national sin, which became such an exit to Israel (Ezekiel 10–24).

God pleaded with the house of Israel to turn from the tradition of their father's way and return to keeping the commandments.

Israel's grace period expired, and they went into captivity (I Kings 14:15-16).

House of Israel's Captivity

Around 721 B.C., the house of Israel was conquered and soon driven out of their land, homes, and critics.

The Assyrians, or modern-day Germans, took the Israelites into captivity, but the house of Judah stayed (II Kings 17:27).

Israel disobeyed by worshipping other gods, eating unclean food, and failing to keep the weekly and annual Holy Days (Exodus 20:3-4, Leviticus 11, 23).

The house of Israel became known as the Lost Ten Tribes.

Now known by another name and speaking a different language, the Israelites are called Christian nations today, but God Almighty is not King over them.

What is called Christianity is a mixture of doctrine and idols from other Babylonian mystery religions and that which is from God's law is despised or ignored (Ezekiel 20:39-44).

House of Judah Brought Back

The book of Jeremiah talks about Judah's captivity.

Jeremiah was constantly trying to warn them, but Judah refused to listen.

King Zedekiah was the last and final king of Judah.

When the Chaldean armies besieged Jerusalem, the city was broken up, and the palace and the temple were destroyed.

All the king's sons were killed before his eyes, as were all the princes.

King Zedekiah's eyes were put out and he was bound in chains and carried away to Babylon where he died (Jeremiah 39, 52:27-30).

The books of Ezra and Nehemiah are the only books of the Bible that deal with the history of that time.

The house of Judah stayed in captivity for 70 years.

RESTORATION OF THE MARRIAGE COVENANT

I used to think that communication was the key until I realized comprehension is. You can communicate all you want with someone but if they don't understand you, it's silent chaos.
~Anonymous

Let's face it....

Both God's word and man's history make it obvious that we humans have always had problems with authority (Romans 8:7).

Human rebellion is a problem that must be handled within marriage and the family.

Both sexes have contributed to the social problem.

The new morale has progressed so fast that people in general have a confused definition of the word morals.

Sex outside of marriage is now the talk of the town.

The problems children are having today are because of the family.

God has given us the knowledge to break this cycle and recapture true family values.

Three problems in marriage are:

- Selfishness
- Selfishness
- Selfishness

But the fourth is lack of communication.

We might as well have ESP.

In the sixties, during the civil unrest, the automobile could be singled out as one of the most important problems in relaxing the youth's morals.

Automobiles have become mobile bedrooms, a little home away from home, where every form of illicit intimacy can be shared.

Rising numbers of unwed mothers and fathers were having shotgun weddings ending in divorce with miserable lives.

American youth around the world have "experienced new mobility and freedom. Wildly abandoned youth (hippies) have plunged into a swinging new age of sex, pot or marijuana, and the pill.

"Openly flaunting their new freedoms in obscene and defiant fashion," according to Ted Armstrong.

Certain movies are molding the ideas of teenagers such as homosexuality, lesbianism, illicit sex, rebellion against parents and society, crime, and romance.

In this present age, television viewers love sitcom shows.

In the home lively conversations are fading away. Homes are dominated by television, which causes our children to be uncommunicative, lacking intellect, incurious, (not curious), more a prudent of mindless insanity for children on television, which is now the modern-day mother and father for our children. Now, it's our electronic voodoo dolls, we hold in our hand that is magically hypnotic.

Let's face it...

"Sex is in" according to these ill-minded liberal viewers.

According to the study's methods, sexual content included talking about sex, flirting, kissing, intimate touching as well as sexual intercourse.

Part of the reason for the increase is that, in sitcoms, young couples have sex on their minds.

On TV, these young couples have almost nothing but sex on their minds.

Another reason is sex not only sells, but it also sells cheap and easy jokes.

I was watching a special program on HBO on January 25, 2001, called "Sex Bytes."

This program shows different episodes of wild foaming-at-the-mouth sexual fantasies.

The first part shows a female enjoying herself nude on skates jumping out of an airplane.

The second part showed a group called the "Gothics" who believe in sexual worship all around the room.

The third part showed groups having sex on top of the mountain in the green grass while the spirit in the sky was enhancing their sexual dreams.

The other is cybersex, watching sex on computers.

These groupies enjoyed watching new movies on computers.

Last, in Atlanta, Georgia, there was a concert where people dressed up like demonic drag queens, calling themselves the "Snakes."

These sensual pantyhose freaks called their lifestyle universal.

There were gays, lesbians, and heterosexuals in the audience fulfilling their wildest dreams.

This takes us back to God's word when everyone did that which was right in his or her own eyes (Deuteronomy 12:8, Judges 17:6, Jeremiah 10:1-2, Romans 1:26-32).

First and Second Adam

Just believe in Jesus Christ and you shall be saved.

Let's not forget the devil also believes and trembles, Jesus Christ both Son of God and Son of Man.

He was made like unto His brothers yet no sinning.

Going back to the book of Genesis, the Tree of Life represents God's Spirit and the Tree of Good and Evil represents the devil (Genesis 2:8-9).

When Adam took the forbidden fruit, he took to himself the authority to decide right and wrong.

Adam rejected the Tree of Life and brought the death sentence on all humanity (Romans 6:23).

Our Heavenly Father knows that all mankind is on Death Row and needs a Deliverer.

The second Adam, better known as Jesus Christ, took the stand where the first Adam failed.

As God had allowed Satan to test Adam, He now allowed him to test Jesus Christ, but only after Jesus fasted 40 days and nights.

Jesus was able to obey through memorizing of scriptures with the help of the Holy Spirit.

Jesus Christ qualified as the future ruler as King of Kings and Lord of Lords.

The first Adam was disqualified, but the second Adam passed the test.

After repenting with a broken heart and then being baptized, which is the symbol of the death, burial, and resurrection of Christ and receiving the Holy Spirit, God wants us to grow in His spiritual charter daily by loving one another according to His word.

Godly love must be developed which takes time and experience.

That is why we need the Holy Spirit in our lives to grow spiritually mature.

God loved us so much that He gave His only begotten Son as the price for us and, when we look to Jesus, the Author and Finisher of our faith, God the Father will graft us into His kingdom.

We are bought with a price, and we must serve the Lord with all our heart, soul, strength, and mind and love our neighbor as ourselves.

My tongue can do a better job of teasing you than my words can. ~Anonymous
A man that knows how to use his tongue is extremely useful. ~Anonymous

---

Also, life and death is in the power of the tongue (Proverbs 18:21). Why the tongue? I'm glad you asked! It's full of deadly poison and unruly evil. James 3:8 says, "Out of all the creation, the tongue is the most untamable: no human being can tame the tongue. It is a restless evil, full of deadly poison."

In marriage, the tongue can be very beneficial in pleasing your mate. The Song of Solomon explains it all. Song of Solomon 4:11 in the Easy English Bible, "Your lips taste very sweet to me, my bride. They taste like honey that falls from the honeycomb. Milk and honey are under your tongue. The smell of your clothes is like the cedar trees of Lebanon." That's fresh!

Masturbation

We know that more than 70 to 80% women masturbate and 90% of men masturbate, and the rest lie. Some call it wanking, jerking off, shaking hands with the milkman, choking the chicken, etc.

Masturbation gives you that sensational thrilling guilt feeling. Just imagine back in the days of ancient Israel when people had to present different sin offerings to the Temple Priest.

What a job in that area!

They had to keep their minds focused on the job because they had to see a lot of women from different tribes.

Many, many times, the Priests talked amongst themselves daily on their job, striving to obey the Laws of God!

Once a year, the High Priest had to go into the Holy of Holies with a clear mind, including no sexual thoughts because, if he did during that moment, he died!

Imagine living that life!

Let's face the real facts. Humans masturbate whether you want to accept the truth or not! At a young age, when our bodies start developing, we men realize that the toy below our waist have a thrilling sensation besides urinating.

My oldest brother Preston told me that boys have two girlfriends. Their names are Fistina and Palmala. The woman have the finger stirrer and both have additional toys to enhance their gratification.

I didn't know what he was talking about at that point in my life but, as I got older, I saw the light. Most boys and grown men practice masturbation to a greater extent, and the best part about it is you won't to go blind, maybe get arthritis in your wrist as you get older. God knew this and that is why He ordained marriage.

It also can be an almost unbreakable addiction. As parents, we have to talk with our children because, if we don't, the streets will show a different stage.

When I was in high school, my dad bought a book on sexuality. He never told us about sex but wanted us to read the book. I didn't read the book but I enjoyed looking at the pictures every day.

My penis stayed hard in high school every day because I would see the girls at Melrose High School and couldn't wait to get home and look at those pictures again.

Why am I embarrassed? As long as Mom and Dad didn't know what I'm doing, I'm just fine. Thank you very much!

As I've said, there were some things parents didn't talk about in the seventies but, when the streets teach you, it's party time!

Men play with their penis and women play with their clitoris. Many times, we play with our toy until we find out the real reason God designed those parts.

The way God designed it is when the male's lower body is a little lower in relation to his wife's, there will be no contact. In laymen's terms, you are not doing it right! But, if his penis is a little harder to touch the upper part of the clitoris, you hit that gold mine!

God made it for love.

I was doing some research on the woman's clitoris the way God created her. A woman's arousal can be caused by words, sight, smell, thought, and magic touch. The woman is wonderfully made by God. Just don't make her mad because, if you do, there is tribulation in your house.

Sex can be a matter of self-gratification when experienced wrong.

Husbands and wives should ask each other questions on how to satisfy each other and let go, surrendering themselves to each other with whom God has made as one.

Remember to ask questions on what turns each other on because, if you don't, the streets will and somebody might back away and leave their bed and board. If you are not talking with each other, your marriage will get dull and, before you know it, somebody is listening to the wolves in sheep's clothing, whispering, "Talk to me – the dirty stuff. If I can't have you yet, I want you to have sex with me with your voice." ~Anonymous

Soon, there were be arguments to find excuses to leave the household, looking for that itching thrill to satisfy that magnetic pull. It works both ways, so don't see this as a one-sided escape. If there is no passion at home, somebody will tiptoe outside the marriage looking for love in all the wrong places.

Why?

Good question!

Some feel that way maybe from a bad experience a bad experience in the past, their sex drive isn't there no more. Some want a freak or maybe are just holding back those sexual identity struggles. Find out what is wrong before it gets too far out to control!

Take care of your business!

Is Fatherhood Declining?

The more that people surrender to their intimidation, the more fervently they attack the Bible.

Who is really innocent? Matthew 13:15 AMP says, "For this nation's heart had grown gross–fat and dull; and their ears heavy and difficult of hearing and their eyes they have tightly closed, lest they see and perceive with their eyes, and hear and comprehend the sense with their ears, and grasp and understand with their heart, and turn and I should heal them."

For every effect, there has to be a cause! There can be two kinds of knowledge – true or false! Many of these modern watered–down educators have brought us to the point of human extinction by playing "god."

Satan is the god of this world (II Corinthians 4:4). This world or society is deceived in education, service, and religion.

Family is a God–planned relationship. Matthew 19:4,5 AMP says, "He replied Have you never read that He who made them from the beginning made them male and female, and said, for this reason, a man shall leave his father and mother and shall be united firmly (joined in separately) to his wife, and the two shall become one flesh?"

"Marriage, like a garden, takes time to grow. But the harvest is rich unto those who patiently and tenderly care for the ground." Darlene Schach

I didn't say that; it's the Word of God. God created us male and female. We didn't evolve from an ape. We are of the God kind!

Why does man refuse to see his magnificent future? The simple answer is that he doesn't want to be corrected and changed. Our communities in America are struggling with this human parasite called "Hashon hara in Hebrew – evil speech!.

Our young children are growing up in an environment where mothers and fathers are shouting at each other, using foul barbaric language, smoking, and excessive alcohol. When children are exposed to those surroundings, they will imitate that behavior as a normal way of life. Many of our children go to school sleepy and hungry, but only God knows what hell they are going through at home.

Our communities are daily plagued with an increasing crime of every kind, robbery, violence, shooting, assault, rape, murder, drug addiction, alcoholism, perversion, promiscuity, abortion, child abuse, divorce, corporate crime, tax evasion, welfare rip-offs, gang warfare, misguided hoodlums running wild in the streets while fighting the police and intimidating communities, etc.

As modern-day Romans, we need a better solution in our society because human ideology without God isn't working now.

God prophesied through Isaiah that one generation would succumb to rule by women and accept the arrogance and rebellion of ill-mannered youth. Isaiah 3:12 in the Easy English Bible says, "Now children are cruel to my people and women rule over them. My people, your leaders lead you in the wrong direction. They cannot show you what is right."

Isaiah 3:4-5 GNB says, "The Lord will let the people be governed by immature boys. Everyone will take advantage of everyone else, and worthless people will not respect their superiors."

Remember back in the days when you used to lick out our tongue at each other? When our parents or guardians would see us, they would smack our tongues and immediately we would put it back in our mouth? This didn't just start. It's more common now than ever. Not only with our kids, but also with the grown ups. The New Living Translation oof Isaiah 57:4, "When do you mock, making faces and sticking out your tongues? You children of sinners and liars!"

As parents, you have to watch what you do in front of your children and what kind of lifestyle you live. Your children pay attention to everything you do, and they imitate you. It's simple.... Right now, would you want your children to be like you? If your answer is no, then change that behavior. Be a good role model for them.

"When y'all was young, y'all knew that me an your mother would take care of y'all. As y'all gotten older, y'all see that we have flaws, but we made sure y'all went to church and the Bible was taught at home. Put all your trust in God, because we might do something that will cause you to turn away from God," says Dad. Proverbs 2:66 CJB says, "Train a child in the way he (should) go; and even when old, he will not swerve from it."

This is the word of God! I'm not judging anyone because I didn't write the Bible. But I can interpret the Bible my own self-righteous way to fit my ego, but that's vanity.

Our God is a loving Father, but He hates our Bible rejecting Judeo-Christian society with its rebellion, lawlessness, and perversion.

Our God reveals where the ultimate human responsibility lies. He makes it quite clear to you and me that the "buck stops" not with the child, not with the woman, **but with the man – the man, the father,**

husband, and grandfather. This is what we get when we walk away from God.

God is not referring to man's inability to work because of age and health failure. He is focusing on man's failure to fulfill his leadership responsibilities, both to his family and community. The cause of crime is right inside the human home.

How many husbands today are blockheads, lazy, drunks, gluttons, child molesters, wife beaters, unfaithful, deserters, and unwilling to provide for their families and still calling themselves a man? He needs to check his attitude. When a man violates his role according to the Word of God, his children can suffer dearly in this evil society.

Both sexes have contributed mightily to the horrendous social calamity. Women through their rebellion against male leadership and men through leadership that is overly **harsh, or extremely nonexistent**, which goes back to the marriage covenant according to the word of **God!**

I remember many days growing up in Orange Mound in the '70s when my dad would always shoot basketball, throw a football, throw a baseball, or take my brother Percy and I to run track at Melrose Stadium. I remember those moments to this day.

Bernard and our nephew were too little to keep up with us. I do remember Bernard and our nephew got a Chopper for Christmas and many of my siblings would push them to see who was fastest. I always wanted to push Bernard on his Chopper. Our race track was from David to Baltimore.

My Dad was a diehard Cowboys fan. He bought Bernard a Cowboys jacket when he was around four years old. I wanted to be different, so I chose the Pittsburgh Steelers. Dad let me slide with the Steelers, thank God. Dad wanted his family to be Cowboys fans. From Dad's translation 1:1, "I'm going to train y'all to be Cowboys fans except for Courtney. When they get old, they better not depart from my team."

The only time I saw my Dad get soft is when his children were leaving his nest going to the military and college.

Also, he tagged our butts if we were not doing good in school. He wanted the best for his children, while Mom stayed on her knees praying for the whole family. Dad passed away now, but Mom at in her late 80s, still keeps her family lifted in prayer.

According to our constitution, we as Americans have a right to exercise any faith our hearts desire. I studied many sacred religions when I joined the U. S. Army in 1982, but I will always go back to my grassroots in reading with an open mind by showing respect for other faiths and I want the same respect out of brotherly love. I'm very grateful to have had a Dad and Mom in the same house.

DIVORCE

This is a subject that I really hate to talk about because I am in my fourth marriage. My first wife is still living. My second wife and third wife died from heart failure. I am in my fourth marriage and still trying to get it right. Darn!

I mention in my memoir that a baby doesn't make a marriage. I married my first wife because the old folks said, "If you get her pregnant, you have to marry her." That doesn't work all the time. That marriage ended nasty, but we have a loving daughter named Priscilla from all this heartache. Now, since she's older with three kids, she makes sure I take care of myself, especially keeping my colon checked!

Divorces can get nasty and violent, such as in custody battles, child support, DNA, jealousy, kidnapping, and last but not least, death by suicide.

Phrases such as "If I can't have my kids, nobody can" or "May there be a cold day in hell if you think you are going to take my baby (or babies) away from me."

Please count the cost before you say, "I do." By the grace of God, I survived my two nasty marriages.

Does the Bible allow divorce for any reason? There are three reasons for divorce.

1.) **Fraud**—a person can get married for the wrong reasons, such as hating to be alone, entrapment, financial reasons, or he or she may have believed they have finally married a virgin. Go with me to Deuteronomy 22:13-21 MSG, "If a man marries a woman, sleeps with her, and then turns on her, calling her loose, giving her a bad name, saying, "I married this woman, but when I slept with her, I discovered she wasn't a virgin," then the father and mother of the girl are to take her with the proof of her virginity to the town leaders (Juvenile Court) at the gate. The father is to tell the leaders, "I gave my daughter to this man as wife and he turned on her, rejecting her. And now he has slanderously accused her, claiming that she wasn't a virgin. (this man has been around) But look at this, here is the proof of my daughter's virginity." And then he is to spread out her bloodstained wedding garment before the leaders for their examination. The town leaders then are to take the husband, whip him, (Court Fine) fine him a hundred pieces of silver, and give it to the father of the girl (Medical and Family Stress). The man gave a virgin girl of Israel a bad name. (whatever happened in his past relationships, he didn't get away this time). He has to keep her as his wife and can never divorce her." (That is what he deserves for manipulating a sweet innocent precious young lady) (*Now the young lady can go to court, if she is mistreated.*)

NOTE: *I imagine his family embarrassment from family members and so-called friends such as 1. I told you to leave her alone. 2. Drinking that wine and messing with the wrong person cause all these problems for life. 3. Think about the embarrassment of your parents. Maybe his mom is saying, "You are acting like your dad when he was young."*

Continuing with the passage, "But if it turns out that the accusation is true and there is no evidence of the girl's virginity, the men of the town are to take her to the door of her father's house and stone her to death.

She acted disgracefully in Israel. She lived like a whore while still in her parents' home. Purge the evil from among you."

Imagine your only daughter being stoned to death on your front pouch and there's nothing you can do because it's the "LAW"!

"She acted disgracefully in Israel. She lived like a whore while still in her parent's home. Purge the evil from among you."

2.) **Unbelief**—Refusing to believe in God and His Word. I'm speaking from a Bible perspective so please respect me from a neutral perspective...thank you, my lovable readers.

I Corinthians 7:10-15 CSA says, "To the married I give this command—not I, but the Lord—a wife is not to leave, she must remain unmarried or be reconciled to her husband—and a husband is not to divorce his wife. ¹² But I (not the Lord) (His opinion) say to the rest: If any brother has an unbelieving wife and she is willing to live with him, he must not divorce her. ¹³ Also, if any woman has an unbelieving husband and he is willing to live with her, she must not divorce her husband. ¹⁴ For the unbelieving husband is made holy by the wife, and the unbelieving wife is made holy by the husband. Otherwise, your children would be unclean, but as it is they are holy. ¹⁵ But if the unbeliever leaves, let him (her) leave. A brother or a sister is not bound in such cases. God has called you to live in **PEACE** (You can do bad by yourself)."

Now think about this for a moment. The word "unbeliever".... His/her spirituality may be different from you, but you may have known this upfront. But there is a dry spell that is getting rather old. The attitude and the mouth began to change slowly. Maybe because of drugs, alcohol, lack of work, not fulfilling obligations at home, etc. People get tired of all the mess. I see enough of that in the ER. Then, without counseling, it can be ugly. How bad do you want your marriage to work? Try talking to each other and please exercise good listening skills.

If you have read my memoir about my life growing up in Orange Mound, you came across my two nasty divorces. I wanted the perfect marriage if it was done my way according to the Bible. Instead of helping, I was hurting (mentally speaking that is). I realized I caused a big problem and was willing to go to counseling in the first marriage, but by that time, she was long gone.

In my second marriage, she dogged me out. I had to leave that marriage before someone got hurt really badly. Payback is a "M.F." Take it from me – it's as real as the nose on your face.

After my third wife passed away, my second wife wanted us to get back together, but that thrill was long gone. But we did patch up our mess before she passed away. Why does it take someone on a dying bed to make amends? Why?

What does God say about divorce? Malachi 2:16 EEB says, "The Lord God of Israel says this: 'If a man sends his wife away from him, I hate that! He has been cruel to his wife when he should take care of her. So be very careful! Remember your promise to take care of your wife." This is what the Word of God says whether we keep it or not.

3.) Porneia—Fornication or Adultery: It's translated differently in different Bibles. The NASB says Unchastity. The ESB says Immorality. The NLT says Unfaithful. Turn with me to Matthew 19:8-9 GW where it says, " Jesus answered them, "Moses allowed you to divorce your wives because you're heartless. It was never this way in the beginning. ⁹I can guarantee that whoever divorces his wife for any reason other than her unfaithfulness is committing adultery if he marries another woman." NOTE: *It works both ways!*

Listen up fellas, young women want to be loved because of who they are, their likes and dislikes, attitudes, their dreams, and hopes for life. They want to be loved for themselves, not as passersby taken for granted as objects to satisfy the sexual-temporary thrill.

I don't have a dirty mind. I have a sexy imagination.
~Anonymous

But you are saying "I want to get my freak on, but he/she doesn't!!! What shall I do with all these sexual medicines?" You both need counseling with a therapist whether in person or online. You might have a lot of porn magazines and tapes or vice versa.

When you two come together, you come together intimately, who are you thinking about? Your mate or the tapes/magazines or apps? I'm no saint and not even close but trying to do the right thing to keep my wife happy. I'm praying that God gives me the Wisdom to communicate with my wife because she says I don't listen well. (Darn I let that cat out of the **BAG!**) Maybe it's time to listen more since I'm getting gray in different parts of my body.

Turn with me to Hebrews 13:4 AMP where it says, "Let marriage be held in honor (esteemed worthy, precious, that is of great price, and especially dear) in all things. And let the marriage bed be undefiled (kept undishonored); for God will judge *and* punish the unchaste [all guilty of sexual vice] and adulterous."

Sex is Holy! It is the way God created the family but, since the fall of man, all hell has come out and conjured up every crazy imagination that is against the way God designed marriage. Try to look at what I'm saying from a neutral perspective, please.

After the fall of Adam and Eve, marriage has become freakishly righteous so let your love run over because goodness and mercy will follow if you take care of your business at home.

What is marriage?

I see it as a special relationship between a man and a woman, both of whom are old enough and mature enough to strike out on their own to live and work together as a family.

Most, not all, behavioral problems in children are based on marital problems. In my second book entitled, "From Exposure to Evolution," I talked about my life growing up in Orange Mound here in Memphis, Tennessee.

Dad worked in the Post Office on Pendleton and Park Avenue and cut hair on the weekend behind the Tops Barbeque on Lamar. Mom stayed home to take care of all nine of us on David Street.

Preston was the oldest who stayed with our grandmother on Marianna off Southern Avenue. I had a good childhood and the only time my Dad was mad at me was when I came home with Ds and Fs on my report card or if I hit one of my sisters. Please get a copy of "From Exposure to Evolution" by Courtney M. Gardner.

Back to the Marriage Covenant....

We should learn that failure in family relationships is all about passing problems down from one generation to the next. My lovable readers, God has given us the knowledge to break vicious cycles. The devil knows that as he destroys marriage, he also destroys the family.

I Corinthians 7:3-5 GNT says, "A man should fulfill his duty as a husband and a woman should fulfill her duty as a wife, and each should satisfy the other's needs. A wife is not the master of her own body, but her husband is; in the same way a husband is not the master of his own body, but his wife is. Do not deny yourselves to each other unless you first agree to do so for a while in order to spend your time in prayer; but then resume normal marital relations. In this way you will be kept from giving in to Satan's temptation because of your lack of self-control.". (Get your freak on with each other because God said it's Holy in marriage).

A word to the men....

This was one of my biggest problems. I did the talking and I used to expect her to listen to me and not say a word. But we should know this while dating each other but we don't because the sex is all in the way.

The woman is not a punching bag. The way you treat your woman is in turn doing that to yourself because she is a part of you in the relationship – this is another form of self-infliction and our children see this a lot.

What may have worked in the 1940s–60s doesn't always work in today's society.

A word to the women....

Just because he is good in bed doesn't make him a good man. He needs to get off his you know what and pay those bills instead of playing game and raiding the refrigerator saying, "Baby, the bologna and milk is gone. Get a job, you lazy bum and stop blaming the system for everything."

I've learned the hard way in my first and second marriages. That is, here in America, a woman is going to talk and you are not going to stop her. If you make her mad, there will be tribulation in your house.

If the wife is happy, everyone should be halfway happy but no man wants to go home to someone who complains all the time. That's opening the door to him finding a new partner to cheat with – let's not forget he might overindulge with alcohol or drugs that will ease his mind from all the nagging that he, she, or both have caused.

Think about this....

Someone who has a lot of sexual energy can also have a very healing energy at a spiritual level. "The best healer has a lot of sexual energy." (Anonymous)

In my first book entitled, "From Sheltered to Exposure," I talked about my alcohol addiction. Growing up in a strong Christian Pentecostal family, I was taught to live holy, but I didn't know that I had a bad soul until I went to the village in South Korea. I was never really taught about this lifestyle of drinking and clubbing at night. A lot of my money went to pleasure instead of me managing my money. But, staying in the barracks and eating in the mess hall, I said, "What the heck?" Something was hush-hush.

The point that I'm saying is, "When you are in Rome, do as the Romans do." No. When you get entangled in that culture, it can be a part of you... Amen!

When we kick against women on the streets along with transgender people, drug addicts, etc., the majority are out there because of some kind of abuse in their life. In their mind, they are locked in that lifestyle because of their low self-esteem, fear, embarrassment, self-hatred, loss of identity, and the fact that they've given up on life. I've heard many war stories in hospitals, on the street, and in rehab facilities, including my marriage experience.

DAMMIT! Nobody can't talk about nobody because all of us as humans have deep dark closets.

The foundation of a healthy society is the home and a good home is built around a strong family.

There must be an authority in the home.

Your children are not your buddies.

Our children watch all that goes on in the house and they want to make sure that your words and actions match.

My dad was the authority figure and whatever he said was the "law."

With a house full of children, he had to, especially when he was the breadwinner.

In my early teen years, I would always go to my mom for some money.

If she didn't have it, her favorite words to me where, "Go ask your Pappy." I had to make sure that I had the right attitude and hoped to say the right words to get some money out of daddy. And it worked.

Strengthening family ties requires spending quality time together as a family.

I felt that I could talk to my dad about somethings, but not everything.

Why?

Let me explain.

In 1979, when in the eleventh grade at Melrose High School, our English teacher wanted her students to go and purchase the book "Black Boy."

I told my parents that this one teacher wanted us to buy the book for the class.

That Saturday, on a clear sunny day, my mom gave me some money to take the bus and go buy the book.

I walked to the bus stop close to Melrose Stadium, headed to Park and Highland, then took a transfer to Highland and Poplar.

I didn't know where the bookstore was located, but I saw different people coming and going into different stores.

I was outside of my community trying to find a book entitled "Black Boy." I was puzzled in that area.

A truck pulled up to me and this white man said, "You need some help?"

I said, "Yes, Sir. I'm trying to find the bookstore." He was driving a nice shiny truck and was about 200 pounds compared to my 135–140 pound self.

Remember, it was busy in that shopping center on a nice Saturday morning.

The stranger asked, "What's the name of the book?" I looked a little blank.

He asked, "Does your family live close by?"

I answered, "No, Sir. I live in Orange Mound with my mom and dad and brothers and sisters."

He asked, "What do your dad do for a living?"

I answered, "He work for the Post Office, active in the church." I was waiting for him to take me to the bookstore.

I asked him, "What do you do for a living?"

He said, "I take pictures."

I asked him, "What kind of pictures do you take?" He calmly looked at me when I asked him that question.

He said, "I take pictures of boys."

I asked him, "What kind of boys?"

He said, "Naked boys, my friend, and I have them model for me."

I was saying to myself, "He don't talk like Christian."

I asked him, "Do they get paid?"

He said, "Some yes, and some no."

I asked, "Do you have sex with them?"

He said, "Only the pretty ones." I didn't like where this was going.

He said, "I can take you to our business if you like."

I said, "Thanks, ok, Sir, I just need to take a bus and go back home." He didn't sound like a Christian to me and I was ready to go home to my mom and dad.

He unlocked his door and let me out.

I didn't know that I was talking to a child molester on that sunny Saturday where the crowd was so busy. He was nice and polite and I thought he was going to help me out as a friend to take me to the bookstore that I never found.

I took the bus back home and I was so nervous.

My parents never told me about those kinds of people.

This was the fall of 1979 when this happened.

When I made it home mom asked me if I found the book.

If I would have told my mom that I met a stranger who was supposed to help me find a book but instead was trying to persuade me to take pictures and pay for sex, would she believe me?

I was afraid to tell her and my dad.

If I would have told my Pro-Black dad, he would have put me in his car and headed back to that shopping center looking for him.

All my dad had to say was "Point him out!" God's angels were watching over me because I could have been kidnapped, molested, or killed on that Saturday. My parents never told me growing up about these pedophiles and Satanic rituals that involve sex and other vile addictions, which is psychological mind control. I was told in Seminary to beware of the word DIM – Dominate. Intimidate. Manipulate. That leads to desperation.

Desperation leads to indoctrination.

Indoctrination leads to blind ignorance.

Blind ignorance leads to fear.

So many who are married today and are struggling with their sexual identity, which is leading to divorce.

If you want to keep your marriage safe, put on the armor of God.

Ephesians 6:10-13 GNT says, "Finally, build up your strength in union with the Lord by means of His mighty power. Put on the armor of that God give you, so that you will be able to stand up against the Devil's evil tricks. For we are not fighting against human beings, but against the wicked spiritual forms (energy) in the heavenly world. The rules, authoritative, and cosmic powers of this dark age (society). So put on God's armor now! Then when the evil day comes (temptation), you will be able to resist (just say no) the enemies' attacks; and after fighting to the end (as a boxer) you will still hold your ground (a few knockdowns, but get back up and keep on fighting). Read Ephesians 6:14-18 from this translation or any other your mind desires.

God spared me from all that, although I kept it hidden in my mind because of fear.

Also, I felt that, since I was in special education, who would believe me?

Two or three months later, there was a scene on the news where these same grown men were arrested for taking pictures with nude boys!

The thought that came to my mind was, "That could have been me!" Many demons are hidden in our mental closets. These demons could be on the shelf, on the floor, or behind the clothes in y our mental closet. All we have to do is get help to clear up negative energy that is lurking in our mental closets.

This has tortured me mentally since I was fifteen years old and now, at the age of sixty-one, I can finally share it.

Thank God that I had a strong God-fearing family with a mom and dad in the house.

I can say that, but many, many others can't.

As I said earlier, when you see people walking on the strip any place here in America or different parts of the world, you don't know what they went through, but by the grace of God, there goes I.

My parents kept us in worship service and, on Saturday afternoons, we gathered around the table together to pray and enjoy our Sunday meal together with everyday life along with the word of God.

Deuteronomy 11"18-19 TLV says, "Therefore, you are to set these words of mine in your heart and soul. You are to bind them as a sign on your hand, and frontlets between your eyes. You are to teach them to your children, speaking of them when you sit in your house, when you walk by the way, when you lie down and when you rise up."

"If you are not willing to learn, no one can help you. If you are determining to learn, no one can stop you." ~Anonymous

I used to think that the Holy of Holies rested with my family as my dad was the high priest of the family in Orange Mound on David Street.

I never understood how he would talk with us in riddles from time to time but, as I have gotten older, moving from boy to manhood, I slowly began to understand his level of communication.

1 Corinthians 13:11 CJB says, "When I was a child, I spoke like a child, thought like a child, argued like a child,

now that I have become a man, I have finished with childish ways.

Our children need God with them as they face the many challenges of life in this crooked society.

Negative cycles can be broken, but it takes admitting you need help instead of throwing in the towel! That is why I'm glad Yeshua/Jesus fellowshipped with the rejects who wanted healing because the religious folks didn't give a damn. Yeshua didn't "think like they do." And, since He didn't think they do, He was crucified.

I was always told that if you are dating someone, study their family. Learn the likes, dislikes, communication style, and eating habits because there are dark secrets in every family closet, especially if you are human. If you are an alien, that's different.

What are you looking for in a relationship? Are you looking for the perfect flawless mate? I wish you well!

In my young man days, I used to create my own scroll of a perfect God-fearing woman, but after I started club hopping, getting drunk, and lying to stay out of trouble...Heck! I threw the self-righteous scroll away.

In the mid-seventies, around 1975, I was bussed to a school that was not in my neighborhood. I used to look at the white girls as though they were the Barbie dolls in the TV commercials.

Many of us then had the "White is right. Black, get back and Brown, stick around" mentality. I used to think that she was the Lily of the Valley and Bright and Morning Star until I got older. That propaganda isn't true at all! Women are beautiful all over the world. Just don't make them real angry because you will have hell on your hands.

Then I started listening to Malcolm X, the Black Zionist Movement, the Black Panther Party, and many other nationalists from other cultures after I joined the Military.

So, White (Reddish peach) is not right all the time.

Black, get back; the first shall be last and the last first.

Brown, stick around – do you know what you are?!

Under the same constitution, we are entitled to express how we feel about gender.

Thank God for the struggles and the movements of yesteryear!

The believer's talents are not to be laid up for self. They are to be laid out in service. ~Anonymous

---

My sponsor always called me his unicorn. I would ask him why he call me a unicorn.

"I've never seen nobody like you before" was his answer.

Looking on Google, one of three definitions of the word unicorn in the Oxford language is, "something that is highly desirable by difficult to find or obtain." I've always been that happy go lucky kind of guy all my life.

Many times, he would tell me to never look down on one because all of us have our own personal self-inflicted addictions – no matter what it is. That addiction could be any vice your heart craves.

What shook me is when he started quoting Bible verses although he is a spiritual person. He shared Luke 5:31-32 CJB (Complete Jewish Bible) which says, "It was Yeshua who answered them 'The one who need a doctor aren't the healthy but the sick. I have not come to call the righteous, but rather to call sinners to turn to God from their sins.'"

He said, "If you want your life and marriage to succeed, He is the only way. Also, watch out for wolves in sheep's clothing. Always remain causes daily because all it takes is one slip, and you are back where you first started, but it can be seven times worse. That spicy camel's milk can get you in a lot of trouble from time to time." Now I have a new cocktail drink and it's called beet juice and tart cherry juice.

My AA sponsor has always taught me to be honest, open minded, and willing to step out on my convictions.

I believe in the love for God and my fellow men, which is the Ten Commandments of Love.

To those in the gay community, I love you as a brother.

I had two nasty, bloody divorces and my dad told me to evaluate my life, see where I went wrong, and straighten it out.

In 1985, I was in a mental ward for seeking attention in a stupid way of self-hatred.

In this room, I was around at least five individuals who had done stupid things in their lives that lead them to ending up in this facility.

It was all because of their marital problems. They led to them being in the ward – alcohol and narcotics.

When I heard their horror stories, I couldn't imagine this happening to me and I was single.

A lot has happened in my life through the years. I could blame it on the alcohol, but that was still my choice, I am grateful that my mom was praying for me and my dad was worried about me.

That's when my Dad told me that, if I wanted to date outside of my race, to go ahead and just don't come home gay.

Brown, stick around – do you know what you are?!

I'm not against interracial marriage, but get someone on the same level, because looks can be very deceiving.

What am I saying?

I felt like a prodigal after those two divorces, but I had a strong imperfect foundation in the Holy Bible.

My dad was graciously firm and didn't take no mess. Maybe that was the reason I started back dating older women. That's my preference because I was always told I'm an old man in a young man's body! The majority of the women I dated were older.

I'm sticking with the Holy Bible, but as I said, for those in the gay community, I love you as a brother and, please, let's respect one another.

Let's get back on track with marriage....

You're learning more about a person when you go to bed and wake up with them. Take the time to learn each other!

I like to share a few tips for men and women.

Men

1. When thinking of marriage, look for a wife, not someone to replace your mom. GROW UP!

2. Communicate in marriage as freely as you did in dating. Talk about everything.

3. Honor your wife and treasure her as the "weaker vessel." (I Peter 3:7) A good book to read is "Adam Loves Eve: First Fruits of Zion" with Grant Luton and Russ Resnik. After my baby brother passed away, my job gave me time off from work. I asked my fourth wife, Queen, to play some dominoes with

me. She said okay. Queen, my girly girl wife, would talk smack to me and I would just shake it off. But, when I started talking smack, all hell broke loose. She was so mad at me that evening. I told her that I was sorry for hurting her feelings. That didn't work as much. Eventually, I gave her some TLC, flowers, and my debit card. I'm not out of the doghouse again, thank God. My baby bother (RIP) taught me how to play the street way back in the days, but it doesn't work with everybody, especially with Queen. Be careful with your words when you are trying to develop family fun times. Remember all hell can break loose with that one word and how it's used at the wrong unexpected time. I need to write a pamphlet called, "Shut Your Mouth! Don't Stir Up the Water, Dummy!" I've been apart of this self-help program Toastmasters for twenty-five years and Dale Carnegie since after Rose died in 2008. Both programs teach the art of language. My wife, Queen, is my home grammarian. She gets on me from time to time for not pronouncing the ending "s" on my words or other things such as saying "Ask" not "AXE." It gets on my nerves sometimes, but eating a slice of humble pie helps a lot. Sometimes I need to eat the whole pie. Time does bring about a change when gray starts growing in those hidden parts of the body.

4. Dominate but not domineer. Both of you are equal before God. Marriage is 100% each, so that "meet me half way" is bull crap.

Women

1. When thinking of marriage, look for a leader, not a lap dog!
2. Communicate, but don't nag him to death (Proverbs 21:19). In my second marriage, I had to go home drunk from work to have peace.
3. Submit to your husband, except where he would cause you to disobey God.
4. Always remember, "Every wise woman buildeth her house; but the foolish plucketh it down with her hand (Proverbs 14:1). (NOTE: If mom isn't happy, nobody is happy.)

Forty years ago, someone told me that sex is an ego stroker.

I looked at him dumbfounded, trying to understand what he was saying.

He said that going through the emotions, talking freaky and nasty to each other is lovely but, after that orgasm five minutes later, you're back to arguing with each other like porcupines.

My fourth wife, Queen, always tells me that marriage is a life long journey, not something to figure out overnight.

I've always said, "Honestly, how bad do you want your marriage to work?" So, I had to pray to my Creator for wisdom to make my life better in my marriage.

I had to shake the devil off daily to make this marriage work.

I was a functional drunk but it was time for me to stop and get a mentor. Now that junk food demon is something else....

That's why I had to start writing. I wanted to help the generations to come to understand what the world really has for them.... from my perspective.

In my third book entitled, "The Millennial News" on Amazon, I used the W. Cleon Skousen book, "The Naked Communist." I used information from his book to describe our society in general.

All three of my books are on Amazon today!

The scales on your eyes will come off when you read my books:

1. From Sheltered to Exposure
2. From Exposure to Evolution
3. The Millennial News

Go to Amazon!

The devil hates the family of God and is conspiring to destroy you physically and spiritually. He never had an opportunity to be a part of God's family. That knowledge only intensified his hatred.

Revelation 12:12 AMP says, "Therefore, be glad (exalt), O heavens and you that dwell in them! But woe unto you, O earth and sea, for the devil has come down to you in fierce anger (fury) because he knows that has (only) a short time (left.)" What is the new agenda? We will undermine the morale of people in America. "Once there is confusion and after we have succeeded in undermining the faith of the American people in their government, a new group, will take over. This will be the German American group, and we will help them assume power." ~Adolf Hitler, 1933

The great tribulation of World War III is slowly approaching to depopulate the world and control the remaining who are left behind to create the new order of AI.

It's time to stand for God.

God's kingdom will be established, but the sad part is how much man has to suffer before he learns that lesson!

Marriage is like a game of chess. The object of the game is to protect the King. The king can only move one square at a time, but the Queen controls the whole board. The Queen is the most defensive, protective, and the most powerful of them all. A good woman is the same way. That is why teamwork is the only way for a marriage to work in our society.

I watch Animal Kingdom sometimes and I will see how the mom will do all in her power to save and protect her babies even if it costs her life. We can learn a lot by watching the animal kingdom after the fall of humanity.

According to Daniel Mannix's "The History of Torture," Ernest Thompson Seldon gives us "The Ten Commandments in the Animal World," which points out how animals have and maintain ethical standards as far as group preservation, protecting the youth, and mating. Ironically, these correlate to the **last six of the ten commandments followed in Christianity**.

Marriage is a covenant between a man and a woman.

That is why, when you are about to enter a covenant with someone, you both must understand what you are promising to bring to the relationship.

Communication thus becomes of the utmost importance.

Marriage must be built upon trust and respect – without these essentials, no marriage will last very long.

God put the desire in man to love for companionship.

God established order in the marriage.

Today, people have turned from God's order of marriage and have established their own orders.

They now say that same-sex marriages are all right. I know we have our constitutional rights as Americans. The reason I say that is because, in our society, your opinion is your opinion, but the U. S. Constitution has the final say. It sounds rather agnostic, but again, that's my opinion. All of us have the same constitutional rights and we must learn to respect each other. But if we don't stand for something, we will fall for every wind of doctrine.

Women are saying today, "I don't need a man."

We must stay with God's marriage order if we want our marriages to be happy.

The wife is more interested in romance and tender touches.

The husband should complement her with flowers and tell her that he cares and loves her. Women need that reassurance at all times. You can brainwash and control anyone if they are vulnerable. Women are the happiest when they feel loved and have a family. They expect for the man's words and actions to match together in the relationships. This is a biologically inherit trait that can only come from God, not man. Sad to say that women find "bad boys" more attractive than men who are honorable and respectful. Many women dog out good guys and many men dog out good women because of their past experiences or what they have witnessed in the family home. After two bloody and nasty divorces, I became cold toward young women and started treating them like dirt with a hypocritical smile. But, my life changed when I met Rose. We can make changes in our lives when God sends the right person at the right unexpected time.

My big sister told my brother Percy and I in the seventies, "If you let a woman run over you, you ain't s---." I was in junior high back then and I never bothered to ask her why. A woman goes out and finds a bad boy who talk a lot of sweet nothing. Later, she gets pregnant and the sweet talking bad boy who is irresponsible. She looks for a respectful cake man to take care of someone else's kids. He'll help pay the bills, buy food, clothes, and whatever so he can enjoy her cake and ice cream. Soon, he will say, "Been there. Done that," and move on to another victim if they're vulnerable.

So, she is stuck relying on the government to be her new husband. Then, the whole world is mad at her when she decides to be a lesbian, bisexual, or just have a wide variety of sex toys hidden in her closet away from her children.

Why?

He refuses to step up to the plate to take care of their responsibilities. He put her in that situation by talking nasty while the good guy was just too plain and dull.

We must learn to work with our balance, caring, and sharing.

We must deal with each other according to knowledge and understanding (I Peter 5:7).

In marriage, "the husband belongs to the wife and the wife belongs to the husband."

Adultery violates the sanctity of the marriage union.

Even if one is faithful physically to his or her spouse, a married person must not have romantic feelings for someone else. Avoid making comparisons – keep it to yourself!

The apostle Paul gives a beautiful illustration of how marriage is meant to be in Ephesians 5:22-33.

In conclusion, the Bible's Doctrine of Marriage Covenants is best explained and defined in the scriptures of the Holy Bible. So please respect my views on Marriage according to my Sacred text.... The Holy BIBLE.

Dr. Bilal Philips said, "Both partners in marriage should treat one another in a kind fashion in order to maintain a harmonious atmosphere in the home."

When a bitter woman takes over the house, the family she rules is doomed.~Family Proverb

Talmud, Bava Metziz 59a said, "A person should always be careful about the honor of his wife, for blessing is found in a person's home due to his wife."

"A good marriage isn't something you find, it's something you make, and you have to keep making it." ~Unknown

My readers, I'm only sharing my experience of my perspective of the word called "Marriage", that's all.

When I was 19 years old, I was stationed in Korea, right before I realized that I had a bad side.

One of my sergeants on post enjoyed talking with me about the Bible.

He told me a story that I have never forgotten.

He said, "Private Gardner, listen to this story. You finally met the woman of your life. Your wife and Mom wanted to go fishing together for the first time. You are looking from a distance as they are having the best time ever. Unexpectedly, the boat flipped over and they are fighting to stay alive. You see them from a distance screaming. You can only save one, so who will you save?"
I was speechless from that question.

He said, "The answer is easy, Private Gardner, you will say your wife!"

I said, "I don't understand, Sergeant."

He said, "Just think. When you were a baby, Mom took care of you through all your hunger, aches, pains, and tender loving care as a Mom. Now, as a grown man, your wife will take care of you through all of your hunger, TLC, and being there for you. It also goes both ways for a woman meeting her husband in the same story. Dad has always been there for her as a little girl. Her husband and Dad are fishing in the boat and it flipped over. She can only save one. She will save her husband. Dad wants the best for his little girl. Dad took care of her. Now, it's time for her husband to take care of her." I understood his story as I got older from my trials and errors.

Life changes from young to old the same as the days change from sunrise to sunset.

Maybe that's part of being a greenhorn about life.

One evening, my manager asked me a question that almost had me speechless

He asked me, "What is it like to lose your wife?" That was a table topic question. That really threw me for a loop! At that moment, I prayed for some wisdom from God without choking up. Working in the Trauma Unit and seeing all that goes on, one after the other. Many survive and many don't survive. Loved ones are looking for answers. But when death has knocked on your door to take a family member, that is when it really hits home.

I also told him that, if you went through a nasty divorce, it does hurt bad. But, when you love someone from your heart, that's different. Sometimes, we can worship our mates, which can be a form of idol worship, which is wrong.

There is a void when losing your mate if you love them.

There is a sense of loneliness.

That physical connection is gone.

That is why God said, "It isn't good to be alone." You begin to miss those little things that were taken for granted.

Many "whys" and "if onlys" began to pop in your mind. You have invested time to learn each other and now it's gone.

Now you are waking up and going to bed alone.

Some take it out with drugs or alcohol, feeling like they are young again. They're chasing after another replacement and all they want is your insurance money – 401K, IRA – if you have any money!

Many develop dementia and dwell in the past.

I had to learn that it's going to get better, but when?

I had to stay in God's word and focus on my family who was still alive.

Bill collectors still wanted their money on time.

I had to keep pushing forward because somehow someway, things are going to work out.

I had three choices are losing my wife:

1. I could start looking at porn and masturbate until I get tired.
2. Go on a dating site or look for a trick fix on the street for one-night stands that will ruin your bank account. (I'm too cheap.)
3. Put it all in God's hand and praying that God will send me another mate to fill in that void.

Number three worked better for me.

As my Mom would always say to her children, "Keep the Lord before you!"

As you get older, you want someone to grow old with. We love to hear about the better, richer, and health, but we don't want to talk about the worse, poorer, and sicknesses. All of this comes from the Tree of Good and Evil in the Garden of Eden.

The late John Lennon wrote the song, "Grow Old with Me." I made an attempt to sing this song to Queen during our wedding reception, but I never got a chance to complete the song from all the screaming.

There is a stanza in the song that says, "Grow old along with me. Whatever fate decrees. We will see it through. For our love is true. God bless our love."

"Fate decrees" refers to the idea that a predetermined fate controls the events that happen in life. Death is our ineluctable (inseparable) fate."

Count the cost before getting married.

Have a strong spiritual life and help each other grow together instead of saying, "I quit!"

Take care of yourself and each other.

God bless!

SEVEN STEPS TO A SUCCESSFUL MARRIAGE

Put God first
He is the foundation, the base, the beginning
Do this first
For a successful marriage that will last without ending
Communication is key
To keep a marriage sustained, just remember
To talk it out then love and respect will be gained
Trust one another
Even when it seems hard to do with trust in your foundation
The big problems are easier to get through
Have Forgiveness
In your heart alone with love, faith and trust
Forgiveness
Should come easily. Remember forgiveness is a must
Listen to each other
Right or wrong You may find
That you've agreed all alone

<u>*Touch each other frequently*</u>
Be it a hug or a kiss, It's those little moments
You should not remiss
There's so much more
That makes a marriage work
But practice these seven steps
And the rest will be a perk

By: Tamara Flemings

ABOUT THE AUTHOR

Courtney M. Gardner is a Member of the San Antonio Elks Lodge #216, Grand Chaplain of the Most Worshipful Hiram Abiff, Grand Lodge and Senior Warden of King Solomon #1 under the leadership of WM Patrick Bowman.

He also completed the eighteen hour Citizen Police Academy training, has been a member of Toastmasters International for over twenty-four years, and has been through the Dale Carnegie program.

He credits his wife, Minister Queen Gardner, for her loving support and keeping him in line.

He enjoys reading, writing, exercise and health reform while passing his time playing chess and spending time with his family. One of his favorite magazines is the monthly "Square Magazine" from the U.K.